PUFFIN BOOKS
EEKS! I SAW A COCKROACH!

Arthy Muthanna Singh is a children's writer, freelance journalist, copywriter, editor and cartoonist. She has authored more than thirty-five books for children. Currently, she is a partner at Syllables27, an outfit that produces books for children on a turnkey basis for publishers and organizations that work with children.

Mamta Nainy is a children's writer, editor and translator based in New Delhi, whose book *A Brush with Indian Art* won The Hindu Young World-Goodbooks Award 2019 for Best Book (Non-Fiction).

Charulata Mukherjee studies painting at the College of Art. She can be found sketching silly things all the time—in coffee shops, in the metro, at home—and her sketchbook is her biggest source of entertainment. She loves illustrating for children, especially because she believes that children can see in her illustrations what most adults can't.

About the Series

It's time to enter the fascinating
kingdom of insects with WWF India's
EEKS series! From bees to flies, from ants to
wasps and from mosquitoes to cockroaches, the
books in this unique series will introduce you to
a vast variety of insects we share our planet with
and help you discover some jaw-dropping facts
about them. So, what are you waiting for?
Bug out, have fun and be prepared
to be amazed!

....

is about to
enter the
amazing world of
insects!

PUFFIN BOOKS

USA | Canada | UK | Ireland | Australia
New Zealand | India | South Africa | China

Puffin Books is part of the Penguin Random House group of companies
whose addresses can be found at global.penguinrandomhouse.com

Published by Penguin Random House India Pvt. Ltd
7th Floor, Infinity Tower C, DLF Cyber City,
Gurgaon 122 002, Haryana, India

First published in Puffin Books by Penguin Random House India 2021

Text and illustrations copyright © World Wide Fund for Nature-India 2021

ISBN 9780143451006

Layout and design by Aniruddha Mukherjee
Typeset in Bembo Infant by Syllables27, New Delhi
Printed at Aarvee Promotions, India

www.penguin.co.in

EEEEEEKKKS!

I SAW A
COCKROACH!

Arthy Muthanna Singh and Mamta Nainy

Illustrations by Charulata Mukherjee

PUFFIN BOOKS
An imprint of Penguin Random House

EEEEEEKKKS!

I went to the kitchen
And what did I see?
EEKS!—a cockroach,
As big as can be!

I said, 'What are you doing,
Turning and running away?
After nibbling at my biscuit,
What have you to say?'

What are the four words you think
of when you see a cockroach?

1. ....

2. ....

3. ....

4. ....

BOO!
Did you know that the fear of cockroaches is known as katsaridaphobia (cat-sar-id-a-pho-bia)?

MEET THE
COCKROACH

Neel was one of the most popular children in the neighbourhood. He was kind and brave. Brave? Well, everyone thought he was. But he was scared of something after all—only one thing— and if he remained careful, he was sure no one would find out.

One day, after he had won the badminton match in his neighbourhood, he brought three of his teammates home for a snack. His parents were not at home. They were out for their daily walk. So, Neel brought out biscuits, juice and apples. But he couldn't find his favourite corn chips. He opened all the cupboards, but no luck.

'Help me,' he called out to his friends. 'Can't find the corn chips.' His friends came to the kitchen.

Anita opened the kitchen cabinet and out jumped a cockroach on to her hand! 'EEKS!' she screamed, almost falling down.

'Arghhhh!' shouted Sid, dropping the biscuit as he moved quickly away.

'Ewwww!' Neel almost fainted.

But Reeta! She didn't scream. She didn't move. Because she was NOT scared of the cockroach at all.

'Why are you all so scared of this tiny little creature?' she asked her friends.

'Tiny little creature?' her friends exclaimed, shocked. 'This tiny little creature of yours is creepy!'

'No, it's not!' said Reeta. 'Cockroaches aren't creepy, cockroaches are cool. Let me tell you how!'

COCKROACHES AREN'T CREEPY!

Yes, you read that right. Cockroaches aren't creepy at all. In fact, these little animals are some of the coolest creatures of the insect kingdom. They are wonderful recyclers! Did you know that? Most kinds of cockroaches live outdoors in the wild and eat dead leaves and other organic matter. They turn them into fertilized soil that plants need to grow. The few kinds who live close to people eat up all that we waste—leftover food, trash and even soap. And that's not all! There are many more supercool things about cockroaches that might help you think differently about them. Read on to find out!

Guess how many different kinds of cockroaches there are on this planet? A whopping 4500! (You must be wondering how researchers know this . . . Well, there are insect experts who keep track of the number and the types of cockroaches discovered.)

But most of these cockroaches live in forests, caves and burrows. Only about thirty species of cockroaches like to live where people do. And you may only see about four of these in your homes.

A WORLD OF BUGS

If you become an entomologist when you grow up, what animal would you study?

This rare blue beauty of the genus *Eucorydia* can be found in China..

OLDER THAN DINOSAURS

I magine you're a time traveller. You step into your time machine and zoom right back in time—some 300 million years ago. Suddenly there's a loud sound. Your robot announces that you're about to land.

This beautiful cockroach of the genus *Trilobite* can be found in wooded areas, forests and gardens.

Your machine comes to a sudden stop. You open the door and step out. You see plants and trees around you. But you don't see any dinosaurs. And of course, there are no humans. You look down and you see something moving. What do you think it is? A cockroach!

Cockroaches have been here on Earth for a very, very long time! And what's even more amazing is that they have not really changed much. In prehistoric times, female cockroaches had a sharp organ shaped like a tube that helped them dig the ground. Then they laid their eggs. Cockroaches today do not have that organ. Also, the cockroaches that we see today have wings that look a little different from the cockroaches in earlier times. But oevrall, cockroaches' bodies are very similar to how they were millions and millions of years ago!

BUG NINJAS
Cockroaches can hold their breath for up to 40 minutes!

A cockroach's body is flat, oval-shaped and wax-coated. The wax makes its body waterproof and that's why it can stay in water for ten to fifteen minutes without drowning. A cockroach's outer body is also very hard. It protects it from its enemies like a suit of armour. And, like most insects, its body is divided into three main parts—the head, the thorax and the abdomen.

Two pairs of wings— forewings and hindwings

Flat, oval body— perfect for squeezing into tiny spaces

Two pointed barbs at the back called cerci. The hair on the cerci can sense tiny changes in the air current, signalling possible danger.

Tiny holes on the sides of the body called spiracles to breathe

Three pairs of legs with five joints each—to help quick movements

9

If you have ever tried to chase a cockroach, you would know how quickly it can escape! It can slip through a crack no wider than a matchstick, and one of the main reasons for this is its body shape.

Dr Kaushik Jayaram and Dr Robert Full, scientists at the University of California, Berkeley, got so inspired by the cockroach's flat body shape and jointed shell that they created a similarly designed robot that could help in search and rescue efforts! Isn't that amazing?

Meet CRAM, A ROBOTIC COCKROACH!

EXOSKELETON

Cockroaches, like all insects, are cold-blooded. They don't have a skeleton the way we do, i.e., inside the body. Instead, they have what is called an 'exoskeleton'—a hard exterior shell that protects what's inside. When they grow, they shed their exoskeleton and grow a new one!

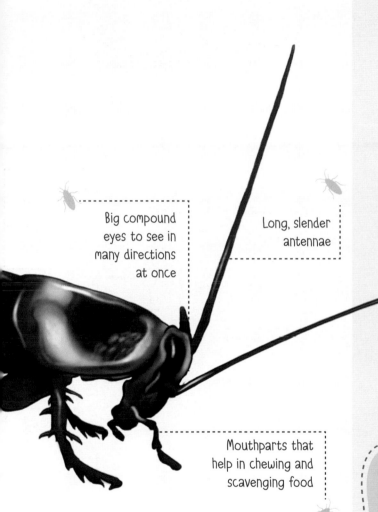

Big compound eyes to see in many directions at once

Long, slender antennae

Mouthparts that help in chewing and scavenging food

PARTS OF A COCKROACH

IT'S A COCKROACH'S LIFE!

How long does a cockroach live? Well, on an average, a cockroach lives for about a year—as long as it keeps getting food, water and air. But some cockroaches live longer than others. For example, the Madagascar hissing cockroach can live up to 2 to 5 years! The life cycle of a cockroach starts with the production of eggs. Cockroaches are actually baby-making machines! Before becoming a mama, the female cockroach gives off an especially nice smell (pheromones) that the male cockroach would find attractive. This means she wants him to be the papa to her babies.

After mating, a female cockroach stores its eggs in a protective casing called ootheca (oh-uh-thee-kuh), inside her body. It then squeezes out this egg case—depositing it somewhere or carrying it on its back until the eggs hatch. Once the eggs are ready to hatch, the female cockroach either hides the case or drops it. The newly hatched cockroaches are called nymphs. The nymphs grow by shedding their hard outer shell or exoskeleton as they grow larger, until they are fully grown.

Believe it or not, cockroaches live in groups, exactly like a family! And now the fun part—some studies have also shown that cockroaches have personality traits, just like humans! Some can be shy and cautious while others may be confident explorers. So if you find a cockroach exploring your kitchen even when the lights are on, you now know what its personality trait is!

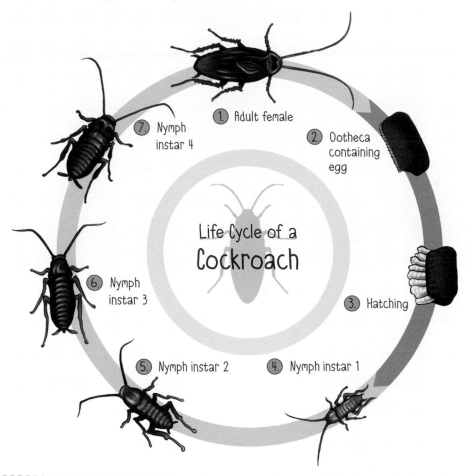

Life Cycle of a
Cockroach

1. Adult female
2. Ootheca containing egg
3. Hatching
4. Nymph instar 1
5. Nymph instar 2
6. Nymph instar 3
7. Nymph instar 4

The newly hatched cockroaches, or nymphs, shed their skin multiple times until they're fully grown. The process of shedding the skin is called moulting and the period between each moult is called an instar.

OF MANY KINDS

Just like humans, cockroaches are also of various kinds. Some are big, some small. Some are drab, some colourful and bright. Some are outgoing, and some extremely shy. Like humans, they have also adapted to living *everywhere*, except Antarctica. But humans live there too, so can cockroaches be far behind?

Many of the cockroaches found in the wild are much bigger than their cousins who live where humans do. The heaviest known cockroach in the world, the rhinoceros cockroach, weighs a whopping 35 g. That's about the same as the weight of two tennis balls! Found in Central and South America, another cockroach species, *Megaloblatta longipennis*, has the longest wings—from tip to tip, they measure about 8 inches, the size of an unsharpened pencil. And then there are also cockroaches who hiss like snakes!

DOMINO COCKROACH

Also called desert cockroach, it's mostly found in south India. It can grow up to 30 mm, lives in the leaf litter in scrub forest habitat and is active at dawn and dusk.

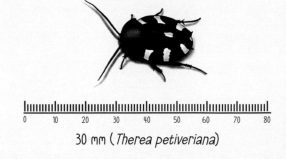

30 mm (*Therea petiveriana*)

MADAGASCAR HISSING COCKROACH

One of the largest species of cockroaches, it can grow 50–75 mm. To scare off intruders and attract mates, it makes a hissing sound by firing air out of the tiny holes along its body. Where can they be found? In Madagascar, of course—mostly under rotting logs.

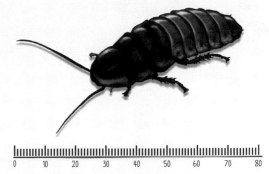

50–75 mm (*Gromphadorhina portentosa*)

RHINOCEROS COCKROACH

Also called giant burrowing cockroach, it grows up to 75 mm and is the heaviest cockroach in the world! It is smooth and shiny and has no wings. It is not a pest and, in some countries, it is even kept as a pet. It can be found in the forests of Australia and is an important forest recycler.

75 mm (*Macropanesthia rhinoceros*)

GREEN BANANA COCKROACH

Also called cuban cockroach, it's a small cockroach— the males are about 12 mm long and the females can grow up to twice that size. It lives among shrubs, trees and leaves and is a pretty green colour.

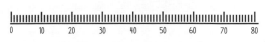

12–24 mm (*Panchlora nivea*)

Cockroaches found mostly in the wild.

COCKROACHES EVERYWHERE!

Now let's read about the most common species of cockroaches found in India and in most parts of the world. They know that they will find enough food where humans live, and so they live wherever we do. You can find them living in the cracks in walls, some very tiny spaces, in basements and garages, inside cupboards, under sinks, places where the plumbing enters walls and leads up to washing machines and even in drains and pipes! And what's more, because we use so many pesticides to get rid of cockroaches, over the years, the pesticides have stopped working on them. So we now have super-cockroaches!

 ## ORIENTAL COCKROACH

Also known as the waterbug or black beetle, this almost black cockroach can mostly be found in dark, damp areas like sewers and drains. It can grow 20–27 mm and has a large, shiny body. It's a scavenger that eats almost anything. The female is wingless while the male has short wings.

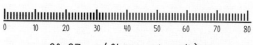

20–27 mm (*Blatta orientalis*)

AMERICAN COCKROACH

The largest species of common cockroach found in sub-tropical regions throughout much of the world, it is reddish brown in colour and can grow up to 40 mm. Often found in dark areas like sewers and drains, it eats just about anything, including plants and other insects. It has a special pattern on the back of its head that looks like the number 8.

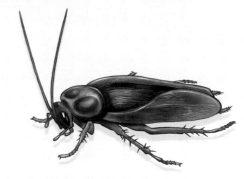

29–40 mm (*Periplaneta americana*)

BROWN-BANDED COCKROACH

It gets its name from its brown colour and the two distinctive lighter bands it has across its dark brownish body. It measures about 10 to 14 mm but has extended antennae that make it appear much longer. It prefers warm and dry locations and can be found in kitchen cabinets, cardboard boxes and under the furniture.

10–14 mm (*Supella longipalpa*)

GERMAN COCKROACH

Brown to dark brown in colour, it has two parallel streaks running across its body. It is about 13 to 16 mm in length. It loves heat and humidity and can mostly be found in kitchens and bathrooms. It's fully winged but rarely flies.

13–16 mm (*Blattella germanica*)

Cockroaches found mostly indoors.

THE SPEEDY SCUTTLERS

Imagine walking into your kitchen in the middle of the night to get a midnight snack or a glass of water . . . And suddenly you feel a tickle on the top of your foot. It's a dark-brown cockroach crawling across your big toe! But just as you are about to shake it off, you find that the creature has already disappeared. That is because you just met one of the fastest scuttlers of the insect world! They move sooooooooooo quickly!

But how do cockroaches do this? How do they sense danger? Do they have something like a sixth sense? Surprise, surprise—it's their hair! According to scientists, the tiny hairs on a cockroach's legs act as sensors.

THE GREAT SPRINTER

The American cockroach is one of the fastest insects in the world. Its top speed is 3.4 miles per hour!

These hairs can sense changes in wind movement and the cockroach is gone! And all this happens in a second!

COCKROACHES ARE GOOD!

Cockroaches are one of nature's waste disposal superheroes and our environment needs these little guys for so many reasons. For starters, here are a few.

1. Cockroaches eat organic waste and, in the jungles, they chew up dead plant and animal matter. This helps make the soil rich. You will be surprised to know that in some countries such as China, they actually breed cockroaches to get rid of the food wasted in restaurants!

2. Cockroaches are gardeners too and some of them help spread seeds in the soil. A few species of cockroaches even pollinate flowers, which helps plants make seeds and fruit. They are important in the food chain; many other creatures eat them!

21

3. Cockroaches are a source of protein for humans, so cockroach milk may become the new superfood! Some scientists have found that a milk crystals produced by the Pacific beetle cockroach, found in Australia, is full of fats, sugars and protein and could be super nutritious for humans too. It could even be better than cow's milk.

4. In many countries, cockroaches are popular snacks. They're nutritious and high in protein.

5. Scientists are also studying some chemicals found inside cockroach bodies that might help make new medicines for fighting bacteria.

COCKROACH FARMING IS A THING

Do you know that, in China, cockroaches are harvested for medical benefits? Yes, that's true! In China, cockroaches are bred because they are believed to be a miracle drug that can cure a number of diseases.

COCKROACH HANG-OUTS!

So, while our planet does need these helpful little insects, we need not invite them into our homes. Just like all the other animals, cockroaches also grow and reproduce when there is enough food and good hiding places for them. Cockroach species that prefer human habitation can usually be found in dark and lonely places to live in. They also love warm and wet places like bathrooms, sewage pits and drains. Sometimes cockroaches can be found inside corners of cupboards, hanging upside down, out of sight. Gymnastics! When cockroaches live among humans, they can spread diseases. The easiest way to prevent them from entering your home is to keep it clean. Bay leaves and neem leaves are some of the things that cockroaches don't like.

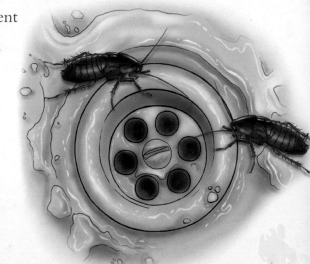

This Cape Mountain cockroach, or *Aptera fusca*, is a large cockroach found in the Western Cape region of South Africa.

If you have these things in your kitchen, you can put them to use! Also, by allowing harmless common house geckos (lizards) to share our homes, we can keep the cockroach population in check.

But most cockroach species live in forests and can be found in dark places—scurrying beneath rocks and logs, across the forest floor, in leaf litter or trees. There are some other species that live in caves, fields, swamps and grasslands. And one species of cockroach can even live in the desert!

Eurycotis Decipiens, also called the Zebra cockroach because of the stripes that it has on its body.

WHAT COCKROACHES LIKE AND WHAT THEY DON'T

LIKE	DON'T LIKE
Warm, cosy and moist environments	Bright sunshine and clean, well-lit places
Dark places like underground burrows, hideouts along the forest floor, tree holes, under rocks and logs, caves, fields, swamps and grasslands	Fast-flowing water
All kind of things, from soaps to books to garbage to hair to paper, to chew on, but they especially like sweets, meats and starches	Creatures who prey on them, like birds, rats, mongooses, centipedes, ants, frogs, lizards, snakes and scorpions
Dirty dishes, leftover food, trash	The smell of peppermint, lavender and eucalyptus
Decaying and dead plant and animal matter including leaf litter, nectar, fruit, bark	Cockroach repellents and other harmful chemicals

THE CUTE COCKROACHES

So now you know that cockroaches don't mean any harm. They just want to live a peaceful life, with enough food and in comfortable environs. They sound much like us humans, don't they?

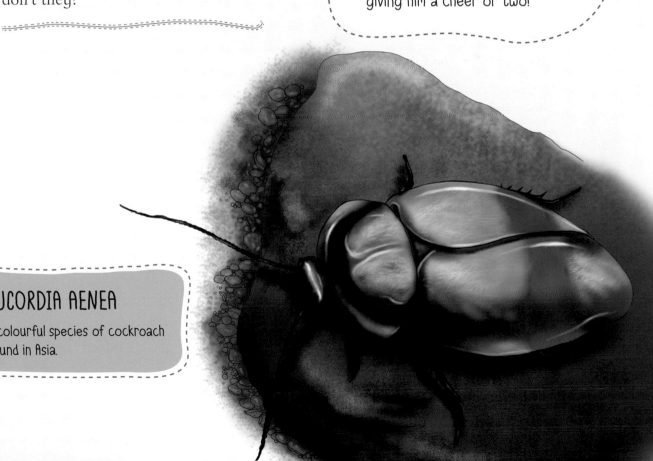

EUCORDIA AENEA
A colourful species of cockroach found in Asia.

COCKROACHES ARE COOL!

So cockroaches don't really deserve an EEKS, do they? Now, write four things that you think are amazing about cockroaches.

1. ....

2. ....

3. ....

4. ....

HARLEQUIN COCKROACH

Found in the tropical areas of the world, it has beautiful patterns on its back.

SOME FUN WORDS TO KNOW ABOUT COCKROACHES

1. **Hindwings**: Back wings.

2. **Invertebrate**: An organism without a backbone—all insects are invertebrates.

3. **Moulting**: Insects grow by shedding their skin multiple times until they reach adulthood; this process is known as moulting.

4. **Nymphs**: Young cockroaches.

5. **Ootheca**: The casing around the eggs of cockroaches.

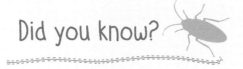 Did you know?

1. A group of cockroaches is called an intrusion.

2. A one-day-old baby cockroach, which is about the size of a speck of dust, can run almost as fast as its parents.

3. Cockroaches are commonly found in homes because they prefer warm environments close to food and water. Unfortunately, cockroaches can cause allergies and trigger asthma attacks. They can also spread different kinds of bacteria.

4. Cockroaches have well-developed senses.

5. One newly discovered species of cockroach has the ability to jump, which is why it is called a leaproach.

CHOCK-FULL OF CRITTER FUN!

Activity 1

Apart from cockroaches, which other insect makes you say EEKS?
Draw and colour it.

Activity 2

Think of a new species of cockroach and name it. Now draw it in the box below. Try it; it'll be fun!

Be a critter spotter!

Our backyards are filled with small fascinating creatures. Go outside and explore the world of insects. Make notes of all the insects that you spot—their sizes, shapes and colours. To help with the exploration, carry a magnifying glass. Make sure you take time to observe. Take photos of the bugs you see or draw their pictures. Write down which bugs you see and where you saw them. From watching a centipede dig in the soil to seeing a bee interact with a flower, there is no limit to the number of things you can discover. But do remember that you're like a giant for a teeny bug—they might get scared of you! Watch them, but don't touch them or pick them up.

More reading on insects

https://kids.nationalgeographic.com/animals/invertebrates/insects/

https://www.si.edu/spotlight/buginfo/incredbugs

https://theconversation.com/birds-bees-and-bugs-your-garden-is-an-ecosystem-and-it-needs-looking-after-65226

https://www.coolkidfacts.com/insect-facts/

https://kids.britannica.com/

Insect Identification Sheet

Date: ....   Time: ....

Draw the insect

Habitat of the insect

Describe where they are generally found in the world

1. How many legs does the insect have?

2. Does the insect have wings?

3. Can you see its eyes?

4. What colour is it?

5. How many body parts does it have?

6. Does it fly, hop or crawl?

Name of the insect: ....

Acknowledgements

We owe a debt of gratitude to the people mentioned below.

Radhika Suri, for showing faith in us, serving as a sounding board for our ideas and navigating our course through the development of this series.

Sohini Mitra, for giving the EEKS series another home.

Shalini Agrawal and Aditi Batra for their editorial finesse.

Aniruddha Dhamorikar, Kaustubh Srikanth, Chetna Singh Kaith, Payal Narain and Surbhi Bhadani for their time, expertise and invaluable inputs.

Our wonderful illustrators—Aniruddha Mukherjee, Priyankar Gupta, Charulata Mukherjee and Mistunee Chowdhury—for sharing our enthusiasm and breathing life into the books with their wonderful illustrations.

And, of course, you, dear reader, for reading this book—we hope you enjoy reading these books as much as we did putting them together!

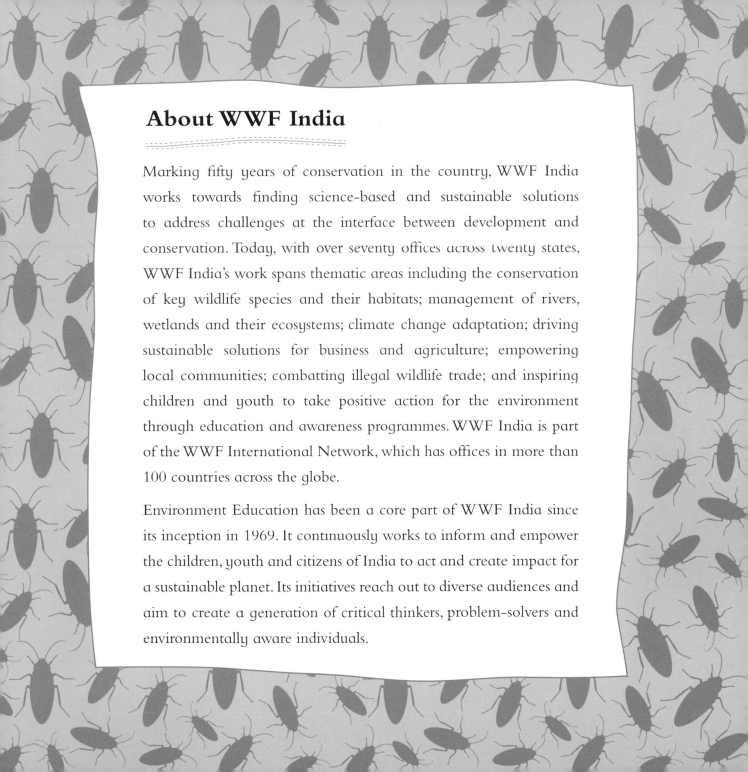

About WWF India

Marking fifty years of conservation in the country, WWF India works towards finding science-based and sustainable solutions to address challenges at the interface between development and conservation. Today, with over seventy offices across twenty states, WWF India's work spans thematic areas including the conservation of key wildlife species and their habitats; management of rivers, wetlands and their ecosystems; climate change adaptation; driving sustainable solutions for business and agriculture; empowering local communities; combatting illegal wildlife trade; and inspiring children and youth to take positive action for the environment through education and awareness programmes. WWF India is part of the WWF International Network, which has offices in more than 100 countries across the globe.

Environment Education has been a core part of WWF India since its inception in 1969. It continuously works to inform and empower the children, youth and citizens of India to act and create impact for a sustainable planet. Its initiatives reach out to diverse audiences and aim to create a generation of critical thinkers, problem-solvers and environmentally aware individuals.

Read More in the Series

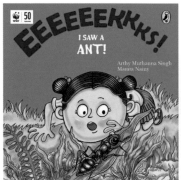  

Ants are small but that's not all! Enter the jaw-dropping world of ants and explore some interesting facts about one of the most hard-working critters of the insect kingdom!

What's the buzz about bees? What do they do all day? Why are they important? Find out everything about bees in this buzzing book and discover the big ways in which these little insects contribute to our environment.

Mosquitoes are mostly known as tiny troublemakers. But there are lots of interesting facts about these delicate insects. Read this book to find out about their many species, sizes, diets, homes and—most importantly—why they bite!